FEELINGS YOU DON'T HAVE WORDS FOR

FEELINGS YOU DON'T HAVE WORDS FOR

TENDER COMICS ABOUT LOVING YOURSELF AND OTHERS

Emu
creator of KAREPANGO!

Andrews McMeel
PUBLISHING®

TABLE OF CONTENTS

LIFE
IS A SERIES
OF STORIES,
BUT WE
NEVER KNOW
THEIR
BEGINNINGS

AUTHOR'S NOTE

This book is dedicated to you, the reader, and whoever you hope to become one day. You can do it.

This book is dedicated to the younger version of myself and all the feelings she couldn't process. I'm sorry you weren't ready to hold yourself.

This book is dedicated to the Karepango team, for believing in my world of imaginary friends.

This book is dedicated to everyone who has touched my life. Thank you for walking with me through the pain, even when you didn't know I was holding it.

This book is dedicated to a future version of myself and all the love she'll be able to hold. I hope she continues to take better care of myself and others.

MEET THE CHARACTERS

MEET THE FRIENDS

KIT

Kit is a lovable mess who aspires to function as an adult. They embody the endless chaos inside us, from unfinished tasks to forgotten texts. Kit is the poster child of "I'm doing my best ... kind of." Kit shows up, even when it's scary, and doesn't pretend to have it all together.

Kit knows being a messy weirdo doesn't make anyone less worthy of love or respect, but they can always use a reminder.

MEET THE FRIENDS

King is the highest version of ourselves. They're the one we look up to for their natural confidence, grounded advice, and compassionate leadership. King has main-character aura, but it's actually sincere. They remain warm, humble, and deeply connected to loved ones.

They represent the kindness and integrity needed to be responsible for others and yourself. King shows up for their people with intention and loves to see others win.

MEET THE FRIENDS

NUB

Nub is the steady, stable friend who you low-key depend on. He doesn't fight for attention and rarely wants to impose, but he probably should. Nub's humble presence witnesses you and all your facets. Nub is a loyal little guy who listens on a hard day, never pushing advice.

His companionship grows on people slowly until he's a constant. Nub embodies the truth that being supportive means sitting in discomfort and holding it all.

MEET THE FRIENDS

NAY & LAY

Nay and Lay are the dueling voices that live rent-free in our heads. They're an odd couple who sometimes create friction but basically balance each other out. Nay is a restless ball of ideas and anxiety; Lay is a calm but stubborn rock. An odd change in mood, environment, or routine can awaken one or the other, which someone else might see as inconsistency.

Nay and Lay are mascots for those of us living with a variety of emotional, mood, or physical changes. The duo represent a radical acceptance and love for all of the voices inside of us. For Nay and Lay, no one is a contradiction, and we are greater than the sum of our parts.

MEET THE FRIENDS

Haya is the friend whose help feels effortless. His energy is grounding and reassuring, always offering perspective when you're under pressure. Haya cheers people on without expecting a compliment in return.

His chill demeanor ends up being a good influence on the friend group. Haya embraces the fact that the best pace is one step at a time and reminds us that "done" always beats "perfect."

MEET THE FRIENDS

YOBI

Yobi is the gratitude that blossoms after sadness. They are a buoyant, curious soul who collects small moments like they are prized trinkets, because everything is worth holding and remembering. Yobi loves memories in the form of ticket stubs, pebbles, or kind sticky notes on the mirror.

Yobi embodies the joy that comes from seeing the beauty in scary things, like the future. Healing is rarely a straight line. They may have no clue what will come next, but they are ready to find joy in the unexpected.

MEET THE FRIENDS

Toro is the love and labor that goes into care. Inspired by Emu's background in Japanese hospitality, Toro carries a tight-knit team with warmth and commitment, leading by example and keeping rhythm for the collective.

Toro is the spirit of countless hours practicing one's craft with intention. He also has rad legs and runs the fastest of the bunch.

MEET THE FRIENDS

Pan is the strength of living through the pain. They cry easily, and their soft, sensitive insides are squishy and vulnerable. Still, that doesn't stop Pan from showing up imperfectly.

Pan embodies the version of ourselves who practices hope during hard times, even if it's more like white-knuckling. They remind us that authentic courage comes from softness.

MEET THE FRIENDS

Snarp is the endearingly awkward friend who sticks out. Their determined face and goofy smile strain with effort, like anyone else who has masked their emotions to feel safe.

Snarp embodies befriending your inner world. They hope to integrate body and mind and be uniquely themselves, even when there are few examples to look up to. They know that the path to feeling self-confident involves coexisting with insecurity.

MEET THE FRIENDS

PID, PAD & PUD

Pid, Pad, and Pud are the pride of shared purpose. This plucky trio loves to work together on everything, but it's for the joy of collaborating, not due to codependency. It's like a mini factory in motion: They solve problems in real time and allow each other to learn on the go.

The group is unpredictable, like managing a small business or a project with loved ones. However, if one is behind, the others will wait. If one is ahead, the rest speed up. Like any strong union, it's all for one, one for all.

MEET THE FRIENDS

TRINC, TRUNC & TRONC

Trinc, Trunc, and Tronc are the healing power of art and creativity. These are friends who weather the unique highs and lows of creation. They understand the necessary shifts in skill and imagination and the real-world limitations that shape us.

This trio shows us that each creation has value, and each role has the ability to make a lasting impact. They encourage and inspire each other, even when it feels like there are no new ideas left. They are the feeling of finally meeting your people, a tribute to chosen family.

MEET THE FRIENDS

Ka, Zo, and Ku are the love for shared humanity across communities. They represent a collage of cultures, lifestyles, languages, and stages of life.

This supergroup knows that loving acceptance and a bit of playfulness go a long way in healing disconnection. Ka, Zo, and Ku show us that mutual admiration and respect are keys to lasting peace.

PLEASE
BE KIND
TO YOURSELF.
IT'S YOUR
FIRST TIME
LIVING THIS
LIFE

1. FEELINGS FOR OURSELVES

EMERGING FROM THE COMFORT OF SELF-ISOLATION

GIVING YOURSELF PROPS FOR TRYING

WITNESSING LIFE BURST OUT OF HARD PLACES

STEPPING INTO UNCERTAINTY WITH CAUTION

KNOWING YOUR PAST SELF FORGIVES YOU FOR MOVING ON

ALLOWING THE SUN TO KISS YOUR SKIN

FINDING A SAFE PLACE TO LEAVE ANXIOUS THOUGHTS BEHIND

FEELING LIKE THE ONLY ONE WHO CAN'T MAKE THE LEAP

WHEN YOU CAN'T SEE YOUR OWN IMPACT

HAVING A SAFE FRIEND FOR CRASH OUTS

LET GO
OF WHAT
YOU HAVE
OUTGROWN

CAN'T ARTICULATE THE IDEA IN YOUR HEAD

NOT STOPPING AFTER YOUR SOCIAL BATTERY DIES

BURNING OUT FROM PROCESSING ALL YOUR ANGER

STAYING WHOLE WHEN LIFE WASHES OVER YOU

STARTING TO FEEL AT ONE WITH THE QUIET

SAVORING HOW GOOD THINGS TAKE TIME

THE OVERWHELM FROM A DELUGE OF NOTIFICATIONS

THE COMFORT OF AVOIDING THE STORM OUTSIDE

FEELING STUCK WITH THE SAME MEDIOCRE CHOICES

THAT FIRST TEAR-FALL AFTER HOLDING IT IN

SALVAGING WHAT YOU CAN FROM A MISHAP

NEEDING A SAFE SPACE TO AVOID PEOPLE

HOLDING YOURSELF TOGETHER THROUGH THE PAIN

UNTANGLING YOUR SELF-LIMITING BELIEFS

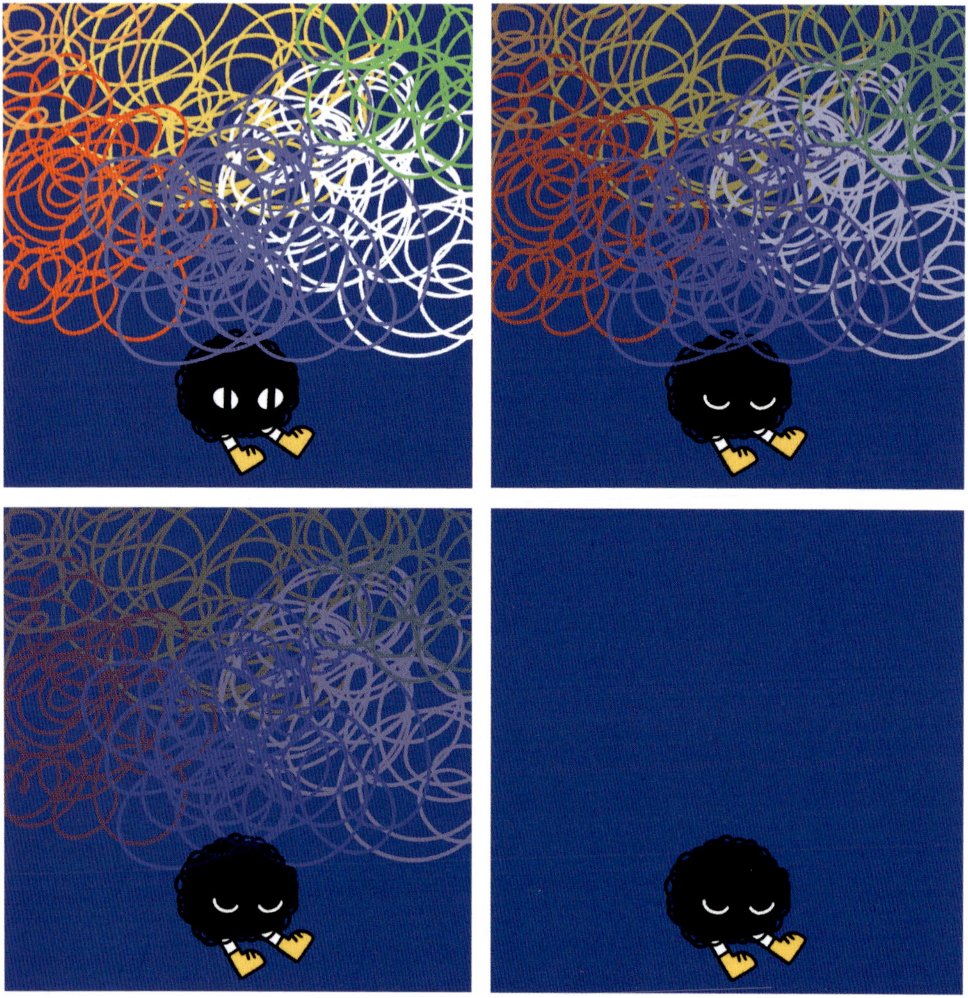

DEADLINES OCCUPYING YOUR EVERY THOUGHT

LEAVING WORK ANXIETY OUTSIDE

PERFECTIONIST HABITS SABOTAGING YOUR IDEAS

PROUDLY COMMITTING TO SLOW PROGRESS EACH DAY

5

MAKING YOUR OWN WHITE NOISE

THE SCARY FIRST STEPS OUTSIDE YOUR COMFORT ZONE

THROWING THE PLAYBOOK AWAY AND TRUSTING YOURSELF

MAKING PEACE WITH THE UNKNOWABLE

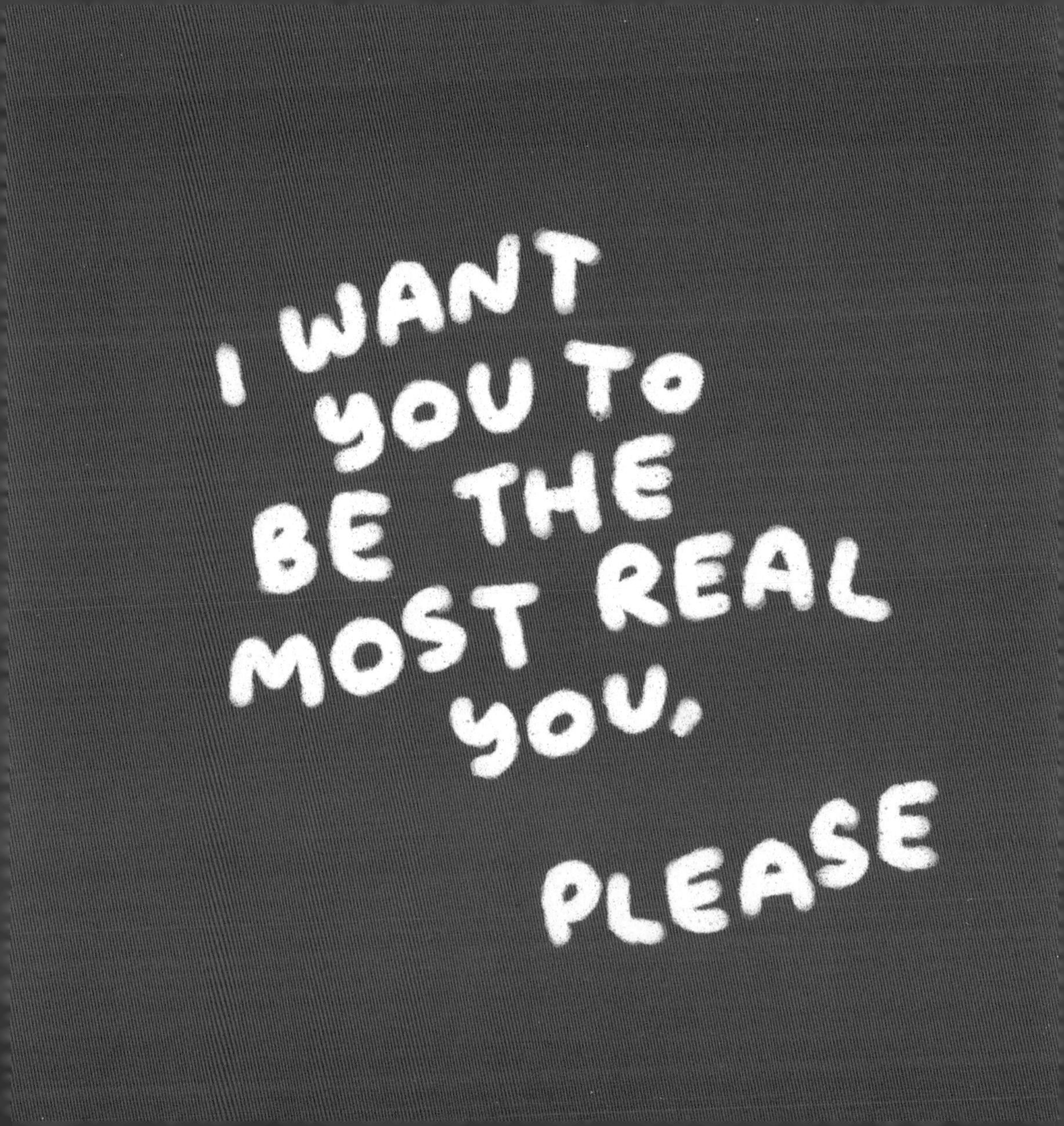
I WANT
YOU TO
BE THE
MOST REAL
YOU,
PLEASE

2. FEELINGS FOR OTHERS

DROPPING THE MASK TO BE VULNERABLE WITH A FRIEND

SITTING WITH SOMEONE, EVEN WHEN THEY'RE ISOLATING

THE JOY OF MAKING AND GIVING A GIFT BY HAND

WHEN IT'S YOUR TURN TO BE THE STRONG ONE

APPRECIATING THE BEAUTY OF BROKEN THINGS

THE JOY OF GIVING YOUR FRIENDS GOLD STARS

SHARING TIME WITH THE PERSON WHO RECHARGES YOUR SOCIAL BATTERY

ALLOWING THINGS TO GROW AT THEIR OWN PACE

THE LONELINESS OF LOSING YOUR SOCIAL CONNECTIONS

LET'S SIT
IN
SILENCE
WITH NO
NEED TO
FILL IT

CELEBRATING OTHERS' WINS FROM THE SIDELINES

1

STRUGGLING TO KEEP A BRAVE FACE

THE BEAUTY OF NATURE STOPPING YOU IN YOUR TRACKS

WHEN YOUR FRIEND'S ADVICE ACTUALLY WORKS

RESISTING THE MOOD TO CELEBRATE

. . . UNTIL YOU'RE SWAYED

FRIENDS WHO STILL SHOW UP AFTER YOU PUSH THEM AWAY

WORKING TOGETHER AND SHARING THE SPOILS

YUM

THE FREEDOM OF SOMEONE LOVING THE REAL YOU

YOU WILL MAKE SENSE TO THE RIGHT PEOPLE

3.

FEELINGS FOR ALL OF US

SAVORING THE SPECIFIC WARMTH OF FRESH LAUNDRY

ALLOWING OTHERS TO CATCH UP AT THEIR OWN PACE

NOT WANTING THE FUN TIMES TO END

SITTING IN SILENCE TOGETHER

FEELING LIKE THE NEW KID IN SCHOOL

STAYING CONNECTED THROUGH THE CONFLICT

REALIZING EVERYTHING WILL BE OKAY, EVEN IF YOU TAKE A BREAK

SLOWING
DOWN
WILL GET
YOU THERE
FASTER
THAN
RACING

HAVING THE SAME EXPERIENCE BUT LEARNING DIFFERENT LESSONS

WHEN THE RELATIONSHIP REACHES TELEPATHIC COMMUNICATION

GETTING THROUGH THE DARKNESS TOGETHER

COMMUNITY EXPANDING YOUR CAPACITY TO LOVE

FEELING LONELY AT THE PARTY

YEARNING FOR A COZY SLEEPOVER WITH BESTIES

ALLOWING EVERYONE'S UNIQUE COLORS TO SHINE TOGETHER

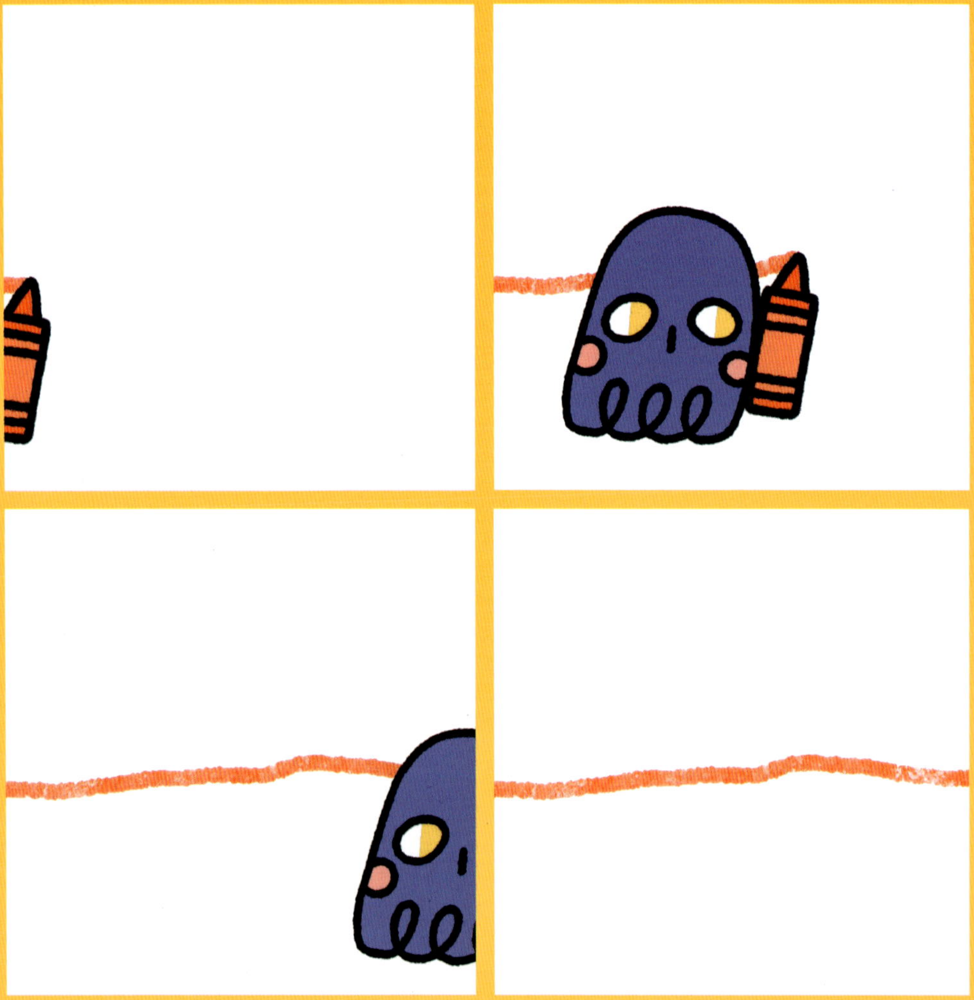

ABOUT THE AUTHOR
EMU

Emu is an artist and entrepreneur driven by the commitment to live her little life with intention. She lived in survival mode for the first twenty years of her life, experiencing major depressive disorder, eating disorders, suicide attempts, and what felt like the longest journey to stability. To Emu, recovery is all about getting back up again and again each day.

She graduated from the University of Chicago and moved to New York City with little else but the hope to build a life of her own. In NYC, she discovered the importance of community in living a life of purpose and intention. She learned to bet on herself. One of those bets was Karepango, her world of imaginary friends. Each character embodies a unique aspect of her experiences in healing: from the joy of hard-won growth to a love for the unanswered questions.

Emu's tiny emotional outlet eventually grew into a brand known for its characters, warmth, emotional honesty, and open invitations for everyone to come as they are. Karepango is the legacy she wishes to leave behind: a haven of acceptance where people's differences are welcomed and understood, and everyone feels a little less alone.

Emu is also the author of *Everything I Leave Behind for You* (2022), a memoir-but-not-quite written to share Emu's difficult lessons in burnout and overwhelm. With *Feelings You Don't Have Words For,* Emu explores how radical vulnerability can quiet the mental noise and remind us of what's real in the here and now.

Look for Emu, her touring dates, and exclusive merch at karepango.com.

Photo Credit: Emu

AFTERWORD FROM THE NATIONAL ALLIANCE ON MENTAL ILLNESS

Karepango + Mental Health Support

Karepango was born from a desire to feel less alone. The characters and stories are inspired by real emotional experiences and the search for connection, belonging, and kindness.

Select Karepango collections directly support the work of **NAMI and other mental health organizations**, helping expand access to education, advocacy, and support for people navigating mental health challenges.

A Note to Readers

This book is meant to offer encouragement, reflection, and a gentle reminder that feelings—especially the ones that are hard to name—are part of being alive. If you're feeling overwhelmed, reaching out to a trusted person or a support organization like NAMI can be a helpful first step.

"If emotions were as simple as happy or sad, life would be much easier. But they aren't—and neither are the people experiencing them.

"In my work, I see every day how often people have feelings they can't yet name, and how powerful it is when someone meets those moments with care. Sometimes we just need permission to not have all the answers—or even the words.

"Nub and Kit embody this so beautifully. *Feelings You Don't Have Words For* reminds us that while emotions can be complex, caring for one another can be simple. It's a quiet invitation into a community where we show up for each other—exactly the kind of community I want to be part of."

—Liz Kahn, MA, MBC

HELPFUL RESOURCES

NAMI HelpLine

The NAMI HelpLine is a free and confidential service available nationwide that provides one-on-one emotional support, mental health information, and helpful resources to tackle tough challenges that you or your family and friends are facing. Self-help online resources are also available through NAMI's website.

The NAMI HelpLine is available M-F, 10 a.m.–10 p.m. ET.

Call: 800-950-NAMI (6264)
Text: Text "NAMI" to 62640
Email: helpline@nami.org

NAMI.org

Learn, connect, and find support groups in your area.

Crisis Resources (US) Available 24/7

Need immediate support, or is someone you know in danger? Help in a crisis is **always** available when you text or call 988 to connect with the Suicide & Crisis Lifeline.

Should I Reach Out?

Built-up stress and trauma can cause a wide range of emotions and responses. These feelings are normal, but they can significantly affect your mental and physical health. If you feel overwhelmed and don't know where to start, it's okay. Contact NAMI HelpLine—they're here to help.

To feel is to be human.

ACKNOWLEDGMENTS

To everyone who ever touched my life, whether it was years ago in a brief impression or you are a trusted support I rely on: I thank you for the time we've shared.

Our lives are never a single story. I am the sum of so many things: unfinished conversations, lessons learned the hard way, wounds slow to heal, endless laughter and kindness, and every goodbye. Each friend, teacher, stranger, colleague, lover, critic, and member of my chosen family has left their fingerprints on my character today.

To the communities that have held me when I did not yet know how to hold myself: Thank you.

To those who believed in me before I could believe in myself: Thank you.

To the Karepango team, who helped co-create this world and fill it with love: Thank you. We're building something larger than ourselves because you invested your faith in the collective.

To the team at Andrews McMeel, who believed in Karepango's whimsical mission to bring joy and belonging to everyone: Thank you for taking a chance with me.

To my partners at Stacher & Stacher, for your exhaustive guidance and support through the evolution of Karepango: Thank you.

Last but not least, to the younger version of me who was tired, scared, and ready to fall into the abyss of despair: Thank you for not giving up. This book exists because you stayed.

With the deepest gratitude, I thank you all.

THANK YOU,
GOODBYE.

The authorised representative in the EEA is Simon and Schuster Netherlands BV, Herculesplein 96 3584 AA Utrecht, Netherlands. (info@simonandschuster.nl)

Andrews McMeel Publishing
a division of Andrews McMeel Universal
1130 Walnut Street, Kansas City, Missouri 64106

www.andrewsmcmeel.com

26 27 28 29 30 RLP 10 9 8 7 6 5 4 3 2 1

ISBN: 979-8-8816-1153-8

Library of Congress Control Number: 2026937937

Editor: Amanda Meadows
Designer: Brittany Lee
Production Editor: Kelsey Rolofson
Production Manager: Chuck Harper

FSC www.fsc.org MIX Paper | Supporting responsible forestry FSC® C102842

DO NOT
THINK
ABOUT IT!
OH NO

YOU LOOK GOOD!
KE IT UP!
DO YOUR BEST!